The Way,
the Truth,
and the Life

DEVOTIONS
ON THE
GOSPEL OF JOHN
FOR TEENS

Book 3

The Way, the Truth, and the Life

ABBY **VAN SOLKEMA**

REFORMED
FREE PUBLISHING
ASSOCIATION
Jenison, Michigan

Reformed Free Publishing
1894 Georgetown Center Drive
Jenison, MI 49428
www.rfpa.org
mail@rfpa.org

Cover design by Erika Kiel
Interior design by Katherine Lloyd / theDESKonline.com

ISBN: 978-1-959515-36-4
Ebook ISBN: 978-1-959515-37-1
LCCN: 2024945528

Therefore being justified by faith,
we have peace with God through our Lord Jesus Christ:
by whom also we have access by faith into this grace
wherein we stand, and rejoice in hope of the glory of God.
—Romans 5:1–2

INTRODUCTION

If you grew up in a godly home, you probably knew from a very young age what it looks like to be a Christian. You saw that church attendance is important. You learned that reading the Bible is vital from learning memory verses and Bible lessons. You received instruction on godly living from your parents and teachers. As you grew older, you began to learn essential doctrines in catechism class.

But do you remember when you realized that simply knowing about God and acting like a Christian wasn't enough? In order to be a true child of God, you must have the gift of faith. You must know and love your heavenly Father personally and trust in him as the only source of your salvation.

Trusting in your own ability to live a life that looks good to other Christians is neither the way to having friendship and fellowship with God in this life, nor in the life to come. Everything that we do is polluted with sin—sin that separates us from our holy God. The only way to the Father is Jesus. He makes the way through his death and resurrection and leads us in this way by his Spirit. There is no other way.

As you read through these chapters of John, pay special attention to the contrast that Jesus shows between the way that leads to life and the way that leads to destruction. Pray that he will show you this way—because you cannot find it on your own apart from God's grace. Let this final instruction of Jesus to his disciples as he prepares to die on the cross remind you that repenting, believing, and trusting in him is the only way to live in true peace; God's word is the only source of absolute truth; and the gift of eternal life is far more important than anything on this earth.

The structure of each day will be as follows: you will first read a passage from John, noting especially the bold-faced verse or verses. Then you will be guided to think about what the passage means by reading the meditation. The "Ask Yourself" section will assist you in applying the truth of Scripture to your life. And finally, the "Praying to Your Heavenly Father" section lists three prayer prompts based on this passage that you can use as a starting point for your own prayer. The journaling space can be used to record your thoughts on the application questions and to write out your prayer.

This volume and the other three in this series are not a comprehensive commentary on the gospel according to John. Rather, they are meant to be a guide to systematically lead you through an entire book of the Bible while familiarizing you with the process of personal Bible study. If you have any questions about the verses that you are reading, I encourage you to talk about them with your parents and siblings, discuss them with godly friends, or go to an elder or pastor for help.

Verily, verily, I say unto you, He that entereth not by the door into the sheepfold, but climbeth up some other way, the same is a thief and a robber.

But he that entereth in by the door is the shepherd of the sheep.

To him the porter openeth; and the sheep hear his voice: and he calleth his own sheep by name, and leadeth them out.

And when he putteth forth his own sheep, he goeth before them, and the sheep follow him: for they know his voice.

And a stranger will they not follow, but will flee from him: for they know not the voice of strangers.

This parable spake Jesus unto them: but they understood not what things they were which he spake unto them.

DAY 1 – **A FAMILIAR SHEPHERD**

In John 9, we read about the religious leaders throwing the blind man Jesus had healed out of the temple for confessing that Jesus was God. Following this incident, Jesus remained in Jerusalem and continued to teach the same group of people—a mixture of both Pharisees and his followers. Here he used the picture of sheep and their shepherd to show that these religious leaders were not leading the people in the right way.

In Jewish villages, sheep from many different flocks were often kept in a large, central pen at night. It was guarded by a porter, or doorkeeper. In the morning, the porter would let each of the shepherds in, and they would call for their sheep. We often think of sheep as being herded in the Western way: by sheepdogs. But in the Middle East, shepherds use unique calls to gather their sheep instead. The sheep of each shepherd would recognize the call and follow him.

Jesus was using this picture of a shepherd calling his sheep to show the close, loving relationship that he has with each one of his children. He knows each one of them, and they know him and follow him. The religious leaders in Jesus' day were not following Jesus' example. They were only concerned with having a position of authority. They did not know the people or care about them. They cared only about themselves.

Following the example of Jesus, your pastor and elders should also know you personally so that they can be your spiritual leaders. It is important to remember that in order for them to know you, they have to have the opportunity to talk to you. Do you leave right after the worship service ends, or do you stay after for a few minutes to fellowship? Do you regularly attend your youth Bible study and other church events? We must understand that our pastor and elders are only men and will never be able to do their work perfectly. But we should thank God for their efforts and encourage them in their work.

ASK YOURSELF...

How could you encourage your pastor and elders in their work of shepherding the church?

....
....
....
....

How could you be more approachable to them?

....
....
....
....

PRAYING TO YOUR HEAVENLY FATHER

- *Praise* God for his wisdom—his infinite knowledge of all things and all people.
- *Thank* him for knowing and loving you personally.
- *Ask* him to be with the leadership of your church and to help them do their work faithfully.

....
....
....
....
....
....
....
....
....
....
....

Then said Jesus unto them again, Verily, verily, I say unto you, I am the door of the sheep.

All that ever came before me are thieves and robbers: but the sheep did not hear them.

I am the door: by me if any man enter in, he shall be saved, and shall go in and out, and find pasture.

The thief cometh not, but for to steal, and to kill, and to destroy: I am come that they might have life, and that they might have it more abundantly.

DAY 2 – **THE DOOR**

Jesus continued to use the picture of sheep to teach the people. But instead of the shepherd, here he presented himself as the door, or gate of the sheep pen. What do doors do? They open to let people in and shut to keep others out. They guard the entrance to something, such as a home. Jesus functions as the door to the household of God. You can enter only on the basis of Jesus' work on the cross for you. He also has the power to open this door to God's elect children and close it to everyone else.

The religious leaders of Jesus' day were trying to lead the people into the sheep pen by attempting to climb over the high stone walls instead of going through the gate. They did not believe that Jesus was the way to eternal life. They thought they could find their own way in, by doing good works or following their own traditions. This is why Jesus calls them thieves and robbers instead of shepherds. They were doing the opposite of what they should have been doing.

Anyone who promises that you can find peace and safety apart from Jesus does not love you. They may say that they do, but they lie. They are trying to lead you down the wrong path—a path that ends in destruction. This could be a church leader who is teaching false doctrine. It could be a friend who is encouraging you to get involved in something that you know is wrong. Or it could be someone that you follow on social media who is leading you away from Jesus.

The only way to peace and safety is by repenting, believing, and trusting in Jesus. He doesn't say here that he is *a* door, but that he is *the* door. He suffered and died so that you could have abundant life (v. 10)! Psalm 23:2 paints a beautiful picture of a shepherd leading his sheep to a safe place of "green pastures" and "still waters" where they can rest and be refreshed. This same care and protection is yours only in Jesus.

ASK YOURSELF...

Are there any influences in your life that are trying to lead you away from Jesus? Talk about it with your parents or another trusted adult.

. . . .

. . . .

. . . .

. . . .

PRAYING TO YOUR HEAVENLY FATHER

- *Praise* God for his eternal, enduring love.
- *Thank* him for showing you the way to eternal life.
- *Ask* him to lead you in the paths of righteousness (Ps. 23:3).

. . . .

. . . .

. . . .

. . . .

. . . .

. . . .

. . . .

. . . .

. . . .

. . . .

I am the good shepherd: the good shepherd giveth his life for the sheep.

But he that is an hireling, and not the shepherd, whose own the sheep are not, seeth the wolf coming, and leaveth the sheep, and fleeth: and the wolf catcheth them, and scattereth the sheep.

The hireling fleeth, because he is an hireling, and careth not for the sheep.

I am the good shepherd, and know my sheep, and am known of mine.

As the Father knoweth me, even so know I the Father: and I lay down my life for the sheep.

And other sheep I have, which are not of this fold: them also I must bring, and they shall hear my voice; and there shall be one fold, and one shepherd.

Therefore doth my Father love me, because I lay down my life, that I might take it again.

No man taketh it from me, but I lay it down of myself. I have power to lay it down, and I have power to take it again. This commandment have I received of my Father.

DAY 3 – **THE GOOD SHEPHERD**

God's people are often compared to sheep in the Bible. Do you know anything about sheep? Sheep are prone to wander and often become lost. Sheep cannot defend themselves from predators. Sheep need someone to guide them to food and water. They also need someone to shear their wool when it gets overgrown and clean their hooves to keep them free from disease. Sheep need a shepherd. Without one, they cannot even care for their own basic needs.

When Scripture refers to God's people as sheep, it is emphasizing our inability to be self-sufficient. We like to wander and go our own way—a way that usually leads to trouble. We do not have the strength to defend ourselves from the attacks of Satan on our own. We are completely dependent on God to supply our daily needs. We are in desperate need of a shepherd so that we can survive.

Knowing our weakness, the Lord sends faithful shepherds to guide and care for his people. But these men are only human and often fail in their duty. Others who are sent to be shepherds of God's people neglect their calling entirely. Jesus called the religious leaders of his day "hirelings." Hirelings were paid to look after the sheep, but they did not actually love and care about the sheep. When danger came, they abandoned the sheep and saved themselves instead. This situation was not unique to Jesus' day. Israel had many bad shepherds in their history.

The many faithful shepherds that have served the people of God through the ages are a picture of Jesus, the good shepherd. The good shepherd knows his sheep personally. He knows the wrong paths that you are prone to wander down and the ways that Satan tries to attack you. He leads you in the right way by his word and Spirit. The good shepherd also loves his sheep. He loves them so much that he is willing to sacrifice his own life to save them. Jesus' sacrificial death on the cross gives salvation to every one of his sheep—including you.

ASK YOURSELF...

What spiritual dangers are you facing right now?

. . . .

. . . .

. . . .

. . . .

How does your good shepherd protect you from these dangers?

. . . .

. . . .

. . . .

. . . .

PRAYING TO YOUR HEAVENLY FATHER

- *Praise* God for his self-sufficiency.
- *Thank* him for his loving care.
- *Ask* him to be with you as you face the "wolves" of this wicked world.

. . . .

. . . .

. . . .

. . . .

. . . .

. . . .

. . . .

. . . .

. . . .

. . . .

There was a division therefore again among the Jews for these sayings.

And many of them said, He hath a devil, and is mad; why hear ye him?

Others said, These are not the words of him that hath a devil. Can a devil open the eyes of the blind?

And it was at Jerusalem the feast of the dedication, and it was winter.

And Jesus walked in the temple in Solomon's porch.

Then came the Jews round about him, and said unto him, How long dost thou make us to doubt? If thou be the Christ, tell us plainly.

Jesus answered them, I told you, and ye believed not: the works that I do in my Father's name, they bear witness of me.

But ye believe not, because ye are not of my sheep, as I said unto you.

My sheep hear my voice, and I know them, and they follow me:

And I give unto them eternal life; and they shall never perish, neither shall any man pluck them out of my hand.

My Father, which gave them me, is greater than all; and no man is able to pluck them out of my Father's hand.

I and my Father are one.

DAY 4 – **SAFE IN HIS HAND**

J esus' teaching after healing the man of his blindness caused mixed reactions from the people. Some believed, while others claimed that he was possessed by a demon. Between verses 21 and 22, some time has passed. When John continues his narrative, Jesus is back in Jerusalem for the feast of the dedication. This was the same holiday that modern-day Jews celebrate as Hanukkah.

Jesus had not yet proclaimed plainly that he was the Messiah to the crowds of people that came to Jerusalem for the various feasts. This was not because he was afraid of controversy or being arrested. Rather, he knew that most of them would not truly understand what he meant. The majority of the Jews thought that the promised Messiah would come to establish an earthly kingdom. But Jesus came to accomplish the will of the Father by suffering and dying for his people. Yet the works he did and the words he spoke clearly showed that he was the Messiah.

Earthly saviors will come and go. They can promise only short-term deliverance from things like sickness, hunger, poverty, and oppression. The promise of the Messiah is different. It is not the promise of an easy life on this earth that is free from suffering. It is the promise of eternal life. This promise is certain. If you have been eternally elected to be a child of God, Jesus is your shepherd. Once you are part of his flock, no one can ever take you away from him.

This truth is called preservation of the saints. Once you are saved, you can never lose your salvation. Your life on this earth will be filled with difficulties. You will face persecution from a world that is increasingly hostile to Christians, that tempts you to give up your faith. You will face trials that will tempt you to doubt God's goodness. You will struggle against your own sinfulness and be tempted to doubt your own salvation. But in all this, you can be confident that when you die, you will go to heaven and spend eternal life with Jesus—free from sin and suffering at last.

ASK YOURSELF...

Have you ever doubted that you were a child of God because of trials you have experienced in your life?

....
....
....
....

How does this passage speak to these doubts?

....
....
....
....

PRAYING TO YOUR HEAVENLY FATHER

- *Praise* God for his immutability—he does not change.
- *Thank* him for the immeasurable comfort that you have as his child.
- *Ask* him to keep you in perfect peace, to keep your mind on him, and to help you trust in him (Is. 26:3).

....
....
....
....
....
....
....
....
....
....
....

Then the Jews took up stones again to stone him.

Jesus answered them, Many good works have I shewed you from my Father; for which of those works do ye stone me?

The Jews answered him, saying, For a good work we stone thee not; but for blasphemy; and because that thou, being a man, makest thyself God.

Jesus answered them, Is it not written in your law, I said, Ye are gods?

If he called them gods, unto whom the word of God came, and the scripture cannot be broken;

Say ye of him, whom the Father hath sanctified, and sent into the world, Thou blasphemest; because I said, I am the Son of God?

If I do not the works of my Father, believe me not.

But if I do, though ye believe not me, believe the works: that ye may know, and believe, that the Father is in me, and I in him.

Therefore they sought again to take him: but he escaped out of their hand,

And went away again beyond Jordan into the place where John at first baptized; and there he abode.

And many resorted unto him, and said, John did no miracle: but all things that John spake of this man were true.

And many believed on him there.

DAY 5 – **A CHARGE OF BLASPHEMY**

When they heard Jesus' claim that he was God, the Jews picked up stones to kill him. In the Old Testament, death by stoning was the punishment for certain serious sins, such as blasphemy. The sin of blasphemy is to disrespect the name of God with your words. God is jealous for his own glory. If any man diminishes this glory, God's justice demands that he be punished. The Jews were saying that Jesus blasphemed the name of God by claiming to be God when he was only a man. This was a false charge, of course, because Jesus is both truly God and truly man—even if the Jews denied this truth.

Jesus' response to them is a bit difficult to understand for us who are not Jews living in his day. Jesus referenced Psalm 82:6, which refers to men who were judges as "gods." In Psalm 82, Asaph was emphasizing the authority that God gave to earthly judges—the right to be seen as gods. Jesus seems to be saying that if it was acceptable to call these men gods, how much more was it right and proper for him, the actual Son of God, to be called God?

Psalm 82 also speaks about God's judgment on men who misused the positions of authority that God gave them by abusing their power. Jesus' words could also have been a warning to the Jewish leaders that God would judge them for misusing their position of authority. Given their extensive knowledge of Old Testament Scripture, they would have known Jesus' implicit reference.

To accuse Jesus of blasphemy was a terrible sin. Jesus' accusers were actually guilty of blasphemy themselves because they were disrespecting God's name by denying the deity of his Son. Jesus' words and works painted a clear picture of who he was. To deny this obvious fact took pointed effort. But that is exactly what the Jewish leaders did. Though their efforts to stone him failed, they tried to have Jesus arrested again. But he escaped and left Jerusalem.

ASK YOURSELF...

How could you fall into the sin of blasphemy by disrespecting the name of God?

....
....
....
....

PRAYING TO YOUR HEAVENLY FATHER

- *Praise* God for his holiness and justice.
- Have you not honored his name as you should? *Confess* this sin.
- *Ask* him to help you use his name with fear and reverence.

....
....
....
....
....
....
....
....
....
....
....

Now a certain man was sick, named Lazarus, of Bethany, the town of Mary and her sister Martha.

(It was that Mary which anointed the Lord with ointment, and wiped his feet with her hair, whose brother Lazarus was sick.)

Therefore his sisters sent unto him, saying, Lord, behold, he whom thou lovest is sick.

When Jesus heard that, he said, This sickness is not unto death, but for the glory of God, that the Son of God might be glorified thereby.

Now Jesus loved Martha, and her sister, and Lazarus.

When he had heard therefore that he was sick, he abode two days still in the same place where he was.

Then after that saith he to his disciples, Let us go into Judaea again.

His disciples say unto him, Master, the Jews of late sought to stone thee; and goest thou thither again?

Jesus answered, Are there not twelve hours in the day? If any man walk in the day, he stumbleth not, because he seeth the light of this world.

But if a man walk in the night, he stumbleth, because there is no light in him.

These things said he: and after that he saith unto them, Our friend Lazarus sleepeth; but I go, that I may awake him out of sleep.

Then said his disciples, Lord, if he sleep, he shall do well.

Howbeit Jesus spake of his death: but they thought that he had spoken of taking of rest in sleep.

Then said Jesus unto them plainly, Lazarus is dead.

And I am glad for your sakes that I was not there, to the intent ye may believe; nevertheless let us go unto him.

Then said Thomas, which is called Didymus, unto his fellow disciples, Let us also go, that we may die with him.

Then when Jesus came, he found that he had lain in the grave four days already.

DAY 6 – **FOR THE GLORY OF GOD**

Soon after Jesus left Jerusalem, he received word that his dear friend Lazarus was very ill. John does not give many details about the relationship between Jesus and Lazarus and his two sisters, but it was obvious that they were close. In the other gospel accounts we read of additional instances where Jesus visited with them at their home in Bethany.

One would think that Jesus would leave right away for Bethany and heal Lazarus. But instead, he waited two days to begin his journey. When he heard the news, his words foreshadowed what he was going to do. He proclaimed that the purpose of Lazarus' illness was not death, but the glory of God. The intentional way that he waited to go to Lazarus' aid was to serve this purpose. He also mentioned that he was glad that he was not there when Lazarus died because healing Lazarus in this way would strengthen the disciples' faith.

Although he had recently left Judea to escape the threat of the Jews, Jesus was not afraid to go back like his disciples were. Just as a man has a certain amount of time in a day to accomplish the work he has been called to do, Jesus had things he had to accomplish during his time on this earth. Part of this calling was to raise Lazarus from the dead. It was imperative that he go to Judea.

By postponing his arrival in Bethany until Lazarus had died and been in the tomb four days, Jesus was displaying the glory of God; he was emphasizing the miracle of what he would do in raising Lazarus from the dead. He was also foreshadowing his own death and resurrection. Jesus was showing the unlimited power that he had as the Son of God—power over even life and death. The same unlimited power is displayed in your life as well. God delights to use your weakness to show his limitless strength. He uses your difficulties to show his abundant mercy and compassion.

ASK YOURSELF...

What does it mean to "glory in your infirmities" (2 Cor. 12:9)?

....

....

....

....

PRAYING TO YOUR HEAVENLY FATHER

- *Praise* God for his unlimited power.
- *Thank* him for the great mercy and compassion that he shows to you.
- *Ask* him to help you see how your weaknesses bring him glory.

....

....

....

....

....

....

....

....

....

....

....

Now Bethany was nigh unto Jerusalem, about fifteen furlongs off:

And many of the Jews came to Martha and Mary, to comfort them concerning their brother.

Then Martha, as soon as she heard that Jesus was coming, went and met him: but Mary sat still in the house.

Then said Martha unto Jesus, Lord, if thou hadst been here, my brother had not died.

But I know, that even now, whatsoever thou wilt ask of God, God will give it thee.

Jesus saith unto her, Thy brother shall rise again.

Martha saith unto him, I know that he shall rise again in the resurrection at the last day.

Jesus said unto her, I am the resurrection, and the life: he that believeth in me, though he were dead, yet shall he live:

And whosoever liveth and believeth in me shall never die. Believest thou this?

She saith unto him, Yea, Lord: I believe that thou art the Christ, the Son of God, which should come into the world.

DAY 7 – **THE RESURRECTION AND THE LIFE**

When Jesus finally arrived in Bethany, Martha greeted him and voiced her disappointment that Jesus had not come sooner. But even in her disappointment, we can tell from her words that she still trusted that Jesus could have healed Lazarus. When Jesus answered by declaring that Lazarus would be raised from the dead, Martha assumed he was talking about his final resurrection in the last day. She did not even entertain the thought that Jesus could raise Lazarus' body from the grave.

Jesus' response to her was, "I am the resurrection and the life." With this statement, he challenged Martha to trust in his power over life and death. He would soon show this power by conquering death and rising from the dead himself. The fact that Jesus is life means that he can give life to those who are dead both physically and spiritually. He can take a dead soul and work new life in it. And one day when he comes again, he will raise our physical bodies and make them immortal. Then we will be able to live with him in the new heavens and new earth in body and soul (1 Cor. 15).

Jesus' challenge to Martha also comes to you today: "Believest thou this?" (v. 26). Do you believe that Jesus is the resurrection and the life? If you do, it will completely change the way you think about sickness, getting older, and death. Scientists and researchers are trying their best to cure every disease, reverse the aging process, and prolong human life. There is certainly nothing wrong with taking advantage of modern medicine. And when we do lose a loved one because of illness or aging, we may grieve that loss. But we must always keep life and death in their proper perspective by remembering that Jesus is the resurrection and the life. We can take comfort in the fact that our whole life, and also our death, are in his hands.

ASK YOURSELF...

What fears about aging or death do you have?

....
....
....
....

How does the truth of who Jesus is calm those fears?

....
....
....
....

PRAYING TO YOUR HEAVENLY FATHER

- *Thank* God for the gift of spiritual life in Christ.
- Have you gotten caught up in unbiblical ideas about health and fitness? *Confess* this sin.
- *Ask* him to help you keep life and death in eternal perspective.

....
....
....
....
....
....
....
....
....
....
....

And when she had so said, she went her way, and called Mary her sister secretly, saying, The Master is come, and calleth for thee.

As soon as she heard that, she arose quickly, and came unto him.

Now Jesus was not yet come into the town, but was in that place where Martha met him.

The Jews then which were with her in the house, and comforted her, when they saw Mary, that she rose up hastily and went out, followed her, saying, She goeth unto the grave to weep there.

Then when Mary was come where Jesus was, and saw him, she fell down at his feet, saying unto him, Lord, if thou hadst been here, my brother had not died.

When Jesus therefore saw her weeping, and the Jews also weeping which came with her, he groaned in the spirit, and was troubled.

And said, Where have ye laid him? They said unto him, Lord, come and see.

Jesus wept.

Then said the Jews, Behold how he loved him!

And some of them said, Could not this man, which opened the eyes of the blind, have caused that even this man should not have died?

DAY 8 – **JESUS WEPT**

As was the custom of the day, many people had gathered to mourn with Mary and Martha and comfort them in their loss. When Jesus approached them, he was troubled. We can tell from John's choice of words that Jesus did not join in the traditional loud wailing that was taking place. Instead he empathized with the grief and loss of those around him and quietly wept to mourn a dear friend. It is possible that he was also thinking about facing his own death in a short time.

Most of John's gospel emphasizes the deity of Jesus, but this passage especially highlights his humanity. Because of all the great works that he did, it is easy to forget that he was still human. He felt human emotions. Death affected him. He felt the loss of his close friend Lazarus. He felt sorrow because of the grief that it had caused Mary and Martha, whom he also loved.

Jesus must be both fully God and fully man. His humanity was a necessity because only a man could die to pay for the sins of his elect people. The fact that our Savior experienced suffering in a human mind and body while he was on this earth shows his great love for us. It also gives us unique comfort. As Hebrews 4:15 says, "For we have not an high priest which cannot be touched with the feeling of our infirmities; but was in all points tempted like as we are, yet without sin." When you are suffering, Jesus knows how you feel.

Hebrews 4:16 goes on to promise that we are able to "come boldly unto the throne of grace, that we may obtain mercy, and find grace to help in time of need." Although Jesus is no longer with us in person on this earth, he dwells in our hearts through his Spirit. He sits at the right hand of God and hears all our prayers. When we bring our troubles to him in prayer, he will answer us in his mercy and grace.

ASK YOURSELF...

What does it mean to "come boldly unto the throne of grace" (Heb. 4:16)?

....
....
....
....

Do you do this?

....
....
....
....

PRAYING TO YOUR HEAVENLY FATHER

- *Praise* God for his tender loving care.

- *Thank* him for sending Jesus to be our sympathetic High Priest.

- *Ask* him to help you approach him in prayer without fear.

....
....
....
....
....
....
....
....
....
....
....

Jesus therefore again groaning in himself cometh to the grave. It was a cave, and a stone lay upon it.

Jesus said, Take ye away the stone. Martha, the sister of him that was dead, saith unto him, Lord, by this time he stinketh: for he hath been dead four days.

Jesus saith unto her, Said I not unto thee, that, if thou wouldest believe, thou shouldest see the glory of God?

Then they took away the stone from the place where the dead was laid. And Jesus lifted up his eyes, and said, Father, I thank thee that thou hast heard me.

And I knew that thou hearest me always: but because of the people which stand by I said it, that they may believe that thou hast sent me.

And when he thus had spoken, he cried with a loud voice, Lazarus, come forth.

And he that was dead came forth, bound hand and foot with graveclothes: and his face was bound about with a napkin. Jesus saith unto them, Loose him, and let him go.

DAY 9 - **A WONDER**

Can you even imagine witnessing the amazing events that are described here? Can you picture the reactions of the people when the stone was taken away from the cave where Lazarus was buried? They expected to see and smell a rotting corpse. But instead, the man that they had placed in the grave dead four days earlier came walking out, very much alive.

What would your reaction be? Shock? Amazement? Wonder? This was one of the greatest of Jesus' miracles. During his ministry he had given new life to many people by healing all kinds of sickness and injuries. But he had raised people from the dead only three times—the widow of Nain's son, the daughter of Jairus, and now Lazarus. Those who witnessed it in person would undoubtedly remember the experience for the rest of their lives. They would have told everyone they knew about what they saw Jesus do.

But as amazing and life-changing as the miracle of bringing someone back to life is, it is only a picture of what Jesus does in the hearts and lives of all his children. When he raised these people from the dead, he was only giving them more time on this earth. Someday they would die again. But when he works new spiritual life in your heart by the power of his Spirit, you are given eternal life!

Do you ever stop to fully appreciate the fact that you were dead in sin and made alive in Christ (Eph. 2:1)? Or do you take it for granted? It is important for believers to regularly stand in awe of what God has done for us. Remembering the wonder of what God has done lifts our eyes up, away from all the distractions of life on this earth, to gaze on our Savior. And remembering that we have been given new life puts everything in proper perspective. It inspires us to praise and worship and reminds us that our God is worthy of all glory and honor.

ASK YOURSELF...

How are you regularly reminded of the amazing, life-changing work that has been done in you?

....
....
....
....

PRAYING TO YOUR HEAVENLY FATHER

- *Praise* God for the riches and depth of his mercy.
- Have you failed to fully appreciate the miracle he has done in your life? *Confess* this sin.
- *Thank* him for making you alive in Christ.

....
....
....
....
....
....
....
....
....
....
....

Then many of the Jews which came to Mary, and had seen the things which Jesus did, believed on him.

But some of them went their ways to the Pharisees, and told them what things Jesus had done.

Then gathered the chief priests and the Pharisees a council, and said, What do we? for this man doeth many miracles.

If we let him thus alone, all men will believe on him: and the Romans shall come and take away both our place and nation.

And one of them, named Caiaphas, being the high priest that same year, said unto them, Ye know nothing at all,

Nor consider that it is expedient for us, that one man should die for the people, and that the whole nation perish not.

And this spake he not of himself: but being high priest that year, he prophesied that Jesus should die for that nation;

And not for that nation only, but that also he should gather together in one the children of God that were scattered abroad.

Then from that day forth they took counsel together for to put him to death.

Jesus therefore walked no more openly among the Jews; but went thence unto a country near to the wilderness, into a city called Ephraim, and there continued with his disciples.

And the Jews' passover was nigh at hand: and many went out of the country up to Jerusalem before the passover, to purify themselves.

Then sought they for Jesus, and spake among themselves, as they stood in the temple, What think ye, that he will not come to the feast?

Now both the chief priests and the Pharisees had given a commandment, that, if any man knew where he were, he should shew it, that they might take him.

DAY 10 – **AN UNINTENDED PROPHECY**

Many who saw the great miracles of Jesus raising Lazarus from the dead believed, but not all. Some of the witnesses immediately ran to tell the Pharisees what Jesus had done. This prompted the Sanhedrin, the Jewish ruling council, to gather and discuss their concerns about Jesus. The majority of these men did not believe that Jesus was the Messiah. Even though he taught openly that he was the Son of God and proved his claim with his miraculous works, they denied and opposed him.

The Sanhedrin was afraid of Jesus. They saw that he had great powers. They saw that many of the people believed in him and followed him faithfully. These leaders enjoyed the power they had over the Jewish people and the certain amount of authority that the Roman government allowed them. Jesus was a threat to their earthly kingdom. They were afraid of the influence that he had on the people. They were also afraid that the Roman government would see him as a potential rebel leader and take away some of the freedoms of the Jewish nation.

Caiaphas, the high priest, presented the obvious solution to their problem. Jesus must be put to death. His proclamation "that one man should die for the people, and that the whole nation perish not" (v. 50) was an unintended prophecy. He thought that Jesus should die to protect the political freedoms of the Jewish people. But Jesus' death would instead save the souls of all of God's chosen people—both Jews and Gentiles.

Caiaphas and the other Jewish leaders placed their own wisdom above the truth of God. But Caiaphas' involuntary prophecy reminds us that God is in control. Jesus' life was in very real danger. Yet he would not allow himself to be taken until the time was right according to God's perfect plan. There are a lot of wicked men in this world who have the power to do terrible things. Yet every one of these men is still under God's control. No man will ever be able to destroy God's church.

ASK YOURSELF...

Do you have any fears about what is happening in the world right now?

....
....
....
....

How does this passage help calm your fears?

....
....
....
....

PRAYING TO YOUR HEAVENLY FATHER

- *Praise* God for his sovereign control over all things.
- *Thank* him for using all the events in history to accomplish the salvation of his people.
- *Ask* him to help you trust in him, even when you are scared about what is going on in the world around you.

....
....
....
....
....
....
....
....
....
....
....

Then Jesus six days before the passover came to Bethany, where Lazarus was, which had been dead, whom he raised from the dead.

There they made him a supper; and Martha served: but Lazarus was one of them that sat at the table with him.

Then took Mary a pound of ointment of spikenard, very costly, and anointed the feet of Jesus, and wiped his feet with her hair: and the house was filled with the odour of the ointment.

Then saith one of his disciples, Judas Iscariot, Simon's son, which should betray him,

Why was not this ointment sold for three hundred pence, and given to the poor?

This he said, not that he cared for the poor; but because he was a thief, and had the bag, and bare what was put therein.

Then said Jesus, Let her alone: against the day of my burying hath she kept this.

For the poor always ye have with you; but me ye have not always.

DAY 11 – **EXTRAVAGANT WORSHIP**

At the beginning of this chapter, John indicates that it was six days before Passover, meaning that it was the last week of Jesus' life on this earth. Almost half of John's gospel is dedicated to this important week—more than any of the other gospel accounts. At this time Jesus attended a dinner in Bethany. He was likely a guest of honor at this dinner since he had recently raised Lazarus from the dead.

In the middle of the dinner, Lazarus' sister Mary gave Jesus a remarkable gift. She poured a pound of "ointment of spikenard" onto Jesus' feet to wash them. Spikenard, a fragrant oil usually used as perfume, was very expensive. A common laborer would have had to save up an entire year's wages to buy such a large amount of it.

Mary's gift was meant to honor the one who had raised her brother from the dead. She humbled herself before him by washing his feet—a task normally reserved for slaves. She even went so far as to use her own hair to wipe off his feet. She poured out very costly oil on him without regard for its cost. Her concern was not for herself, but to show love and worship to her Lord.

Judas Iscariot's response to Mary's act of worship showed that he was only concerned about himself. He was shocked that she would spend so much money on something precious and then "waste" it by pouring it on Jesus' feet. He said it should have been sold instead and the money put in the bag he had for giving to the poor—the same bag from which he regularly stole. But Jesus defended Mary's actions.

Our Lord deserves extravagant worship. The word "extravagant" means to exceed what is reasonable. If there is one area of your life where you should be extravagantly unreasonable, it is the way you worship your heavenly Father—even if that means taking time and resources away from other things that you love. We can never worship him too often or love him too extravagantly.

ASK YOURSELF...

What are you willing to give up to worship God more extravagantly?

....

....

....

....

PRAYING TO YOUR HEAVENLY FATHER

- *Praise* God for his extravagant gift of life in Jesus Christ.
- Have you let your own selfishness keep you from giving God the worship he deserves? *Confess* this sin.
- *Ask* him to work in your heart an increased desire to worship him.

....

....

....

....

....

....

....

....

....

....

....

Much people of the Jews therefore knew that he was there: and they came not for Jesus' sake only, but that they might see Lazarus also, whom he had raised from the dead.

But the chief priests consulted that they might put Lazarus also to death;

Because that by reason of him many of the Jews went away, and believed on Jesus.

On the next day much people that were come to the feast, when they heard that Jesus was coming to Jerusalem,

Took branches of palm trees, and went forth to meet him, and cried, Hosanna: Blessed is the King of Israel that cometh in the name of the Lord.

And Jesus, when he had found a young ass, sat thereon; as it is written,

Fear not, daughter of Sion: behold, thy King cometh, sitting on an ass's colt.

These things understood not his disciples at the first: but when Jesus was glorified, then remembered they that these things were written of him, and that they had done these things unto him.

The people therefore that was with him when he called Lazarus out of his grave, and raised him from the dead, bare record.

For this cause the people also met him, for that they heard that he had done this miracle.

The Pharisees therefore said among themselves, Perceive ye how ye prevail nothing? behold, the world is gone after him.

DAY 12 – **THE LOWLY KING**

Jesus continued to receive attention from many people who heard that he raised Lazarus from the dead. The story spread even farther as the crowds were gathering in Jerusalem for a feast once again. The Sanhedrin responded to this perceived threat by plotting to put both Jesus and Lazarus to death. This was the setting for Jesus' triumphal entry into Jerusalem.

A great multitude of people went out to meet Jesus as he came into the city. They waved palm branches and shouted, "Hosanna: Blessed is the King of Israel that cometh in the name of the Lord" (v. 13). This is a quotation from Psalm 118, one of the songs that the people sang at Passover. Palm branches were a symbol of military victory and nationalism to the Jewish people. The word hosanna means "please save" or "save now." This showed that the people were excited to welcome Jesus as their king, but as a king that would save them from Roman rule.

A conquering king would have ridden into the city on a horse. But Jesus rode in on a lowly donkey instead, fulfilling a prophecy made in Zechariah 9:9. He declared openly that he was the fulfillment of the Old Testament promises but also that he was not the earthly conqueror they were expecting. He would be victorious, but not in the way they anticipated. His first coming was to save his people from their sin. It is not until his second coming that he will conquer all of his people's earthly enemies once and for all.

In a few short days these people who welcomed Jesus into Jerusalem as their king would demand that he be crucified. By rejecting him, they would show that they cared more about earthly salvation than spiritual salvation. When we focus on things like how we look or on perfecting how we appear to others on social media, we are seeking after an earthly kingdom, too.

ASK YOURSELF...

Are you seeking God's kingdom first (Matt. 6:33)? Or are you seeking your own kingdom instead?

. . . .

. . . .

. . . .

. . . .

PRAYING TO YOUR HEAVENLY FATHER

- *Praise* God for working salvation in your heart.
- *Thank* him for being your King.
- *Ask* him to help you honor him as the Lord of your life.

. . . .

. . . .

. . . .

. . . .

. . . .

. . . .

. . . .

. . . .

. . . .

. . . .

And there were certain Greeks among them that came up to worship at the feast:

The same came therefore to Philip, which was of Bethsaida of Galilee, and desired him, saying, Sir, we would see Jesus.

Philip cometh and telleth Andrew: and again Andrew and Philip tell Jesus.

And Jesus answered them, saying, The hour is come, that the Son of man should be glorified.

Verily, verily, I say unto you, Except a corn of wheat fall into the ground and die, it abideth alone: but if it die, it bringeth forth much fruit.

He that loveth his life shall lose it; and he that hateth his life in this world shall keep it unto life eternal.

If any man serve me, let him follow me; and where I am, there shall also my servant be: if any man serve me, him will my Father honour.

DAY 13 – **GLORY IN HUMILIATION**

John tells us that some Greeks who came to celebrate Passover had heard about Jesus. They approached Jesus' disciples and asked to see him. Jesus' response emphasized the importance of this event. Up until this point, Jesus had mentioned repeatedly that his hour was not yet come (2:4; 7:6, 30; 8:20). But now he proclaimed that the time had come. It was time for him to be glorified as the Son of man. It was time for him to suffer and die for his people—both Jews and Gentiles.

Why did Jesus say that he was about to be glorified if he was about to die? He was not talking about glory in the way that man thinks about it. He was not going to receive honor from men for his achievements. His path of glory was the way of the cross because it was the way that God had prepared for him. His glory was in the pain and suffering of his death. By carrying out the Father's will, he was giving glory to God, and therefore, to himself.

Jesus emphasized this point by using the picture of a grain of wheat. One seed of wheat sitting safely up on a shelf in a jar serves no purpose. For the seed to be valuable, it must be planted in the earth so that it can die. It will then grow into a stalk of wheat that has many seeds on it. In the same way, Jesus had to die and be buried in the ground so that he could rise and save his people. Our earthly bodies must also die to separate us from this sinful world. Then they wait in the ground for Jesus to come again and raise them to life everlasting.

What does it mean to hate your life in this world? It does not mean to disregard it as unimportant. It means to see your life as a way that you can bring honor to God instead of to yourself. It means to constantly battle your own sinful nature and to seek to live according to what God commands in his word. To follow Christ is to glory in the imperfection and inevitable death of your physical body, because you trust in the promise of the glorious body that awaits you in heaven.

ASK YOURSELF...

Do you love your life in this world more than you long for heaven?

....

....

....

....

PRAYING TO YOUR HEAVENLY FATHER

- *Thank* God for saving people from all nations—both Jews and Gentiles.

- Have you been living for yourself? *Confess* this sin.

- *Ask* him to help you use your life to glorify him.

....

....

....

....

....

....

....

....

....

....

....

Now is my soul troubled; and what shall I say? Father, save me from this hour: but for this cause came I unto this hour.

Father, glorify thy name. Then came there a voice from heaven, saying, I have both glorified it, and will glorify it again.

The people therefore, that stood by, and heard it, said that it thundered: others said, An angel spake to him.

Jesus answered and said, This voice came not because of me, but for your sakes.

Now is the judgment of this world: now shall the prince of this world be cast out.

And I, if I be lifted up from the earth, will draw all men unto me.

This he said, signifying what death he should die.

The people answered him, We have heard out of the law that Christ abideth for ever: and how sayest thou, The Son of man must be lifted up? who is this Son of man?

DAY 14 – **FOR YOU**

As God, Jesus knew the horror of what awaited him on the cross. As a man, he was troubled in his soul. The idea of the word translated "troubled" here is to be anxious and distressed. It was as if his soul were all jumbled up and unsettled instead of being at peace. These emotions were part of his suffering: he knew that the cross would not be easy to endure, but he also knew that he must endure it for the sake of his people and the glory of his Father.

God the Father was aware of the suffering of his Son. He heard his cry and spoke audibly from heaven. This happened two other times during Jesus' ministry. God spoke at Jesus' baptism and at his transfiguration, and he spoke again now. Jesus said that his Father spoke to remind the people that God would be glorified through what his Son was about to do. Although Jesus' death was for the benefit of his people, it was ultimately for the glory of God.

Have you ever gotten punished for something that you didn't do? How did it make you feel? Can you imagine volunteering to take a punishment for someone else? Can you imagine willingly experiencing pain so that someone else wouldn't have to? Can you imagine giving up your life for someone else? Is there anyone for whom you would be willing to make this sacrifice?

Jesus did this for you. He was troubled in his soul because he was about to die a slow and painful death hanging on a cross for you. He endured humiliation on this earth to pay for your sins. He was going to suffer the unspeakable agony of hell so that you could go to heaven someday. He would cry, "My God, my God, why hast thou forsaken me?" (Matt. 27:46) so that you would never be forsaken by your heavenly Father.

ASK YOURSELF...

What is your response to thinking about what Jesus endured on the cross for you? Are you sorry for your sins?

....

....

....

....

Are you motivated to worship?

....

....

....

....

Are you inspired to share this truth with others?

....

....

....

....

PRAYING TO YOUR HEAVENLY FATHER

- *Thank* God for sending Jesus to suffer and die for your sins.

- Have you taken this sacrifice for granted? *Confess* this sin.

- *Ask* him to help you glorify him in the suffering that you experience, just as Jesus did.

....

....

....

....

....

Then Jesus said unto them, Yet a little while is the light with you. Walk while ye have the light, lest darkness come upon you: for he that walketh in darkness knoweth not whither he goeth.

While ye have light, believe in the light, that ye may be the children of light. These things spake Jesus, and departed, and did hide himself from them.

But though he had done so many miracles before them, yet they believed not on him:

That the saying of Esaias the prophet might be fulfilled, which he spake, Lord, who hath believed our report? and to whom hath the arm of the Lord been revealed?

Therefore they could not believe, because that Esaias said again,

He hath blinded their eyes, and hardened their heart; that they should not see with their eyes, nor understand with their heart, and be converted, and I should heal them.

These things said Esaias, when he saw his glory, and spake of him.

Nevertheless among the chief rulers also many believed on him; but because of the Pharisees they did not confess him, lest they should be put out of the synagogue:

For they loved the praise of men more than the praise of God.

DAY 15 – **THE GIFT OF FAITH**

Jesus knew his short time on this earth was coming to a close. He was about to pass on the work of his earthly ministry to his disciples. With the short time that he had left, he proclaimed the message of the gospel once again with urgency. He warned the people to believe and follow him. But once again, only a small number of people listened to his warning.

Why did so many people reject Jesus? How could someone who had heard Jesus teach in the flesh and witness his miracles firsthand not believe? How could someone who had heard God speak from heaven not believe that this was his Son? John quotes two prophecies from Isaiah (6:9–10; 53:1) to answer this question. These passages remind us that no one can believe unless God has revealed the truth to them. He must change their hearts (John 3:3). If their hearts are not changed, they continue blindly in their unbelief.

It is easy, looking back, to think, "How could they not believe?" But this is prideful thinking. We cannot believe in our own strength. We need the gift of faith. Ephesians 2:8 plainly states, "For by grace are ye saved through faith; and that not of yourselves: it is the gift of God." There is no room for pride in salvation. We cannot be proud of anything that we have done, but only of what God has done in us. He deserves all the glory!

In our pride, we want to be in charge of our own salvation. But we must humble ourselves before our sovereign God. In eternity, he chose who would believe and who would reject him. He determined who each of his children would be before we were even born (Rom. 9:11–13)! This truth is called predestination. Predestination is a difficult doctrine to understand, but it is clearly taught in Scripture. It reminds us just how great our God is. His greatness is unsearchable, which means we cannot fully understand it with our earthly minds (Ps. 145:3).

ASK YOURSELF...

Why do you think it can be so difficult to believe in the doctrine of predestination?

....

....

....

....

PRAYING TO YOUR HEAVENLY FATHER

- *Thank* God for the gift of faith.
- *Praise* him for his kindness in giving you what you do not deserve.
- Do you struggle with the sin of pride? *Confess* this sin.

....

....

....

....

....

....

....

....

....

....

....

Jesus cried and said, He that believeth on me, believeth not on me, but on him that sent me.

And he that seeth me seeth him that sent me.

I am come a light into the world, that whosoever believeth on me should not abide in darkness.

And if any man hear my words, and believe not, I judge him not: for I came not to judge the world, but to save the world.

He that rejecteth me, and receiveth not my words, hath one that judgeth him: the word that I have spoken, the same shall judge him in the last day.

For I have not spoken of myself; but the Father which sent me, he gave me a commandment, what I should say, and what I should speak.

And I know that his commandment is life everlasting: whatsoever I speak therefore, even as the Father said unto me, so I speak.

DAY 16 – **AN URGENT MESSAGE**

These are the last words that John records of Jesus' public ministry. After this Jesus would retreat to the upper room to give personal instruction to his close disciples before he died.

Jesus raised his voice and reminded the people once again of the message that he had been teaching and preaching to them for the entire time he was on this earth.

He reminded them that he is God, and he came into this world as the revelation of his Father. To believe in God, they had to believe in the truth of who Jesus is as well. He reminded them that he had come into this world for the purpose of calling his people out of darkness to the light of salvation. He challenged them to believe in the truth of who he was and reminded them of the consequences if they did not.

This is the message that God had given him to speak. This is also the same message that we are called to bring to the world today—the simple message of the gospel, the good news of who Jesus is. Yesterday we thought about how faith is a gift of grace. God does not need us to save his people. But we also know that he can use our witness as a means to do so. What a privilege it is to be a part of bringing this message of light to those who are lost in the darkness!

Do you think of personal evangelism as a privilege? Or does it seem more like a burden to you? Often the reason we are hesitant to share the gospel with others is because we are too preoccupied with ourselves and have forgotten about what Jesus has done for us. This is really a lack of love for our neighbor. The most important way to show love to someone is to share the life-changing truth of the gospel with him or her. Jesus is coming again soon! That gives urgency to our calling to tell his words to others. Do you feel this urgency?

ASK YOURSELF...

What is one specific way that you can share the message of the gospel this week?

. . . .

. . . .

. . . .

. . . .

PRAYING TO YOUR HEAVENLY FATHER

- *Thank* God for giving his word to show us the truth.
- Have you been lax in your personal evangelism? *Confess* this sin.
- *Ask* for boldness to declare the urgent message of the gospel to those around you.

. . . .

. . . .

. . . .

. . . .

. . . .

. . . .

. . . .

. . . .

. . . .

. . . .

Now before the feast of the passover, when Jesus knew that his hour was come that he should depart out of this world unto the Father, having loved his own which were in the world, he loved them unto the end.

And supper being ended, the devil having now put into the heart of Judas Iscariot, Simon's son, to betray him;

Jesus knowing that the Father had given all things into his hands, and that he was come from God, and went to God;

He riseth from supper, and laid aside his garments; and took a towel, and girded himself.

After that he poureth water into a bason, and began to wash the disciples' feet, and to wipe them with the towel wherewith he was girded.

Then cometh he to Simon Peter: and Peter saith unto him, Lord, dost thou wash my feet?

Jesus answered and said unto him, What I do thou knowest not now; but thou shalt know hereafter.

Peter saith unto him, Thou shalt never wash my feet. Jesus answered him, If I wash thee not, thou hast no part with me.

Simon Peter saith unto him, Lord, not my feet only, but also my hands and my head.

Jesus saith to him, He that is washed needeth not save to wash his feet, but is clean every whit: and ye are clean, but not all.

For he knew who should betray him; therefore said he, Ye are not all clean.

DAY 17 – **CLEANSING BLOOD**

The task of washing someone's feet was considered particularly lowly in ancient Israel. It was reserved for Gentile slaves. If a Jewish man had a Jewish slave, that slave was not even required to wash his feet. It was unheard of for a teacher to ask his disciples to wash his feet. Yet, as he gathers with his beloved disciples for a final time before his death, the Son of God takes this lowly task upon himself.

Jesus removed his clothing and put on the garments of a slave. He humbled himself to show the great love that he had for his people. But this is more than just a lesson in humility. The washing of feet was an act of cleansing. It was a picture of what was about to happen at the cross. God's people would be washed clean from their sin and made pure in the sight of God—not by water, but by the blood of Jesus. Through Jesus' sacrifice on the cross, the guilt of their sin would be washed away.

Peter impulsively protested Jesus washing his feet. Jesus rebuked him. He said that only those who have been washed can be one with him and have a place with him in heaven. It is interesting to note that Judas Iscariot also had his feet washed by Jesus. Yet he did not receive the true washing of sin that this sign pictured.

Baptism is a similar picture of the cleansing power of Jesus' death on the cross. In the same way, every single infant who is baptized is not a child of God. The sacrament by itself does not save. Baptism, like circumcision in the Old Testament, is an outward sign that pictures a spiritual reality. Jesus washed his disciples' feet here as a picture of the washing away of our sins and also the daily washing of sanctification that his Spirit works in us. He graciously gives us these physical signs to help us understand spiritual things that we cannot see.

ASK YOURSELF...

Have you been baptized? What does your baptism mean to you?

. . . .

. . . .

. . . .

. . . .

PRAYING TO YOUR HEAVENLY FATHER

- *Praise* God for the cleansing power of Christ's blood.
- *Thank* him for clearly revealing the truth so that we can understand it.
- *Ask* him to help you love him and walk in a new and holy life.

. . . .

. . . .

. . . .

. . . .

. . . .

. . . .

. . . .

. . . .

. . . .

. . . .

. . . .

So after he had washed their feet, and had taken his garments, and was set down again, he said unto them, Know ye what I have done to you?

Ye call me Master and Lord: and ye say well; for so I am.

If I then, your Lord and Master, have washed your feet; ye also ought to wash one another's feet.

For I have given you an example, that ye should do as I have done to you.

Verily, verily, I say unto you, The servant is not greater than his lord; neither he that is sent greater than he that sent him.

If ye know these things, happy are ye if ye do them.

DAY 18 – **HAPPY TO SERVE**

Jesus' entire life was a lesson to his disciples. He taught them by his words, but also by his actions. One of the last lessons he taught them before he died was about the humble, sacrificial love they should have for one another. Jesus was speaking here to the future leaders of the New Testament church. How should they be Christ-like in their leadership? By being humble servants.

Young men, Lord willing, you will be the head of a home and a family someday. You may also have the opportunity to be a leader in the church by serving as an office bearer. How will you approach this calling with a servant's heart? Young women, Lord willing, you will be given children someday. You will oversee them day to day under the headship of your husband. How will you approach this calling with a servant's heart?

The message the world will tell you will be the opposite of Jesus' message. The writers, influencers, and experts of this world will tell you that aspiring to be a servant is holding you back. They will encourage you to live a life of service to self. Such a lifestyle is extremely tempting, but it will not bring you true happiness in the end. Jesus promises here that if you live in service to others, you will be happy.

How much of your time is devoted to serving others? What is your attitude and response when you are asked to help someone? Practicing a life of service now will help you grow in your service as you get older. If you have spent your teenage years focused only on yourself, you will find it very difficult to change this mindset as you choose a job, get married, and start a family. A life of happy service starts now! It is not something that can wait until you get older.

ASK YOURSELF...

What are some specific ways you can follow Jesus' example of service in your life right now?

....
....
....
....

PRAYING TO YOUR HEAVENLY FATHER

- *Thank* God for sending his Son to humble himself for you.
- Have you been using your time selfishly? *Confess* this sin.
- *Ask* him to show you opportunities to serve those around you.

....
....
....
....
....
....
....
....
....
....
....

I speak not of you all: I know whom I have chosen: but that the scripture may be fulfilled, He that eateth bread with me hath lifted up his heel against me.

Now I tell you before it come, that, when it is come to pass, ye may believe that I am he.

Verily, verily, I say unto you, He that receiveth whomsoever I send receiveth me; and he that receiveth me receiveth him that sent me.

When Jesus had thus said, he was troubled in spirit, and testified, and said, Verily, verily, I say unto you, that one of you shall betray me.

Then the disciples looked one on another, doubting of whom he spake.

Now there was leaning on Jesus' bosom one of his disciples, whom Jesus loved.

Simon Peter therefore beckoned to him, that he should ask who it should be of whom he spake.

He then lying on Jesus' breast saith unto him, Lord, who is it?

Jesus answered, He it is, to whom I shall give a sop, when I have dipped it. And when he had dipped the sop, he gave it to Judas Iscariot, the son of Simon.

And after the sop Satan entered into him.

Then said Jesus unto him, That thou doest, do quickly.

Now no man at the table knew for what intent he spake this unto him.

For some of them thought, because Judas had the bag, that Jesus had said unto him, Buy those things that we have need of against the feast; or, that he should give something to the poor.

He then having received the sop went immediately out: and it was night.

DAY 19 – **BETRAYED BY A FRIEND**

In Psalm 41, David writes that he has been betrayed by someone close to him. This psalm was likely written after his close friend and advisor Ahithophel betrayed him by joining the camp of David's son Absalom. You may remember that Absalom was trying to steal the throne from his father. David poured out his soul to God in this psalm to express the hurt that he experienced from this betrayal.

Psalm 41 is also a prophecy of a similar betrayal that we read about today in John. Judas Iscariot, one of Jesus' close friends and trusted disciples, was plotting to betray Jesus to the Jewish leaders. Jesus quoted this psalm of David to show that Judas was lifting up his heel against Jesus and fulfilling this prophecy (Ps. 41:9). Jesus had just finished washing his disciples' feet, demonstrating the great love that he had for his people. But Judas showed the exact opposite. His betrayal revealed that he only cared about himself.

Have you ever been betrayed by someone? Maybe you confided in a brother or sister, and they told other people what you said. Maybe a friend started spreading rumors about you that were untrue. Maybe an adult that you trusted did something that was wrong. It hurts to experience betrayal. But Jesus knows how you are feeling. He experienced the same pain that you feel. He knows what it feels like to be rejected by someone who was a close friend. You can bring your hurt to him in prayer, just as David did.

God used Judas' betrayal for the good of his people. He can use the betrayal that you've experienced for your good, too. If you have been betrayed by someone, it would be a good idea to talk about it with a trusted adult. If the one who betrayed you is a brother or sister in Christ, an adult can give you advice about following the way of Matthew 18 to reconcile with the one who hurt you.

ASK YOURSELF...

How can you respond to betrayal with humility?

....

....

....

....

PRAYING TO YOUR HEAVENLY FATHER

- *Praise* God for his faithfulness.
- Have you betrayed someone? *Confess* this sin.
- Pour out your troubles to God. *Ask* him to give you comfort if you are hurting.

....

....

....

....

....

....

....

....

....

....

....

Therefore, when he was gone out, Jesus said, Now is the Son of man glorified, and God is glorified in him.

If God be glorified in him, God shall also glorify him in himself, and shall straightway glorify him.

Little children, yet a little while I am with you. Ye shall seek me: and as I said unto the Jews, Whither I go, ye cannot come; so now I say to you.

A new commandment I give unto you, That ye love one another; as I have loved you, that ye also love one another.

By this shall all men know that ye are my disciples, if ye have love one to another.

DAY 20 – **A NEW COMMANDMENT**

After Judas exited the upper room, Jesus was left with only his faithful disciples. What final instructions did he give them as he prepared to leave them? The answer might surprise you with its simplicity. Jesus repeated a command that he had given them many times and had shown them by example throughout his entire ministry. Love one another as I have loved you.

Why then did Jesus call this a new commandment? Even in the Old Testament, the law of Moses contained the commands to love God with all your heart, soul, and might (Deut. 6:5) and to love your neighbor as yourself (Lev. 19:18). How was Jesus' command here any different from that?

The command was not necessarily new, but it was more developed. When Jesus came to earth as a man, he showed love in a new way. He showed love in his personal relationship with his disciples. He even showed love to his enemies and commanded us to do the same (Matt. 5:43–48). He showed the greatest expression of love by laying down his life on the cross for his people.

The new command is to love one another as Jesus loves us. It is to show that we love God by maintaining loving relationships with our fellow believers in the church. It is to show love to our unbelieving neighbors with the hope that they will be drawn out of darkness to the light. It is to show to our friends sacrificial love that mirrors the great love that Jesus showed on the cross. It is to be a people that are characterized by love.

Are you following this command? Would your friends and family describe you as loving? Is your local church known as a group of loving people? Are your unbelieving neighbors or co-workers aware that you are a Christian because of the loving way you treat others?

ASK YOURSELF...

What are some ways that you could improve in showing love to others?

. . . .

. . . .

. . . .

. . . .

PRAYING TO YOUR HEAVENLY FATHER

- *Thank* him for the love that Jesus shows us through his sacrifice.

- *Ask* him to help you reflect this love to those around you.

- Have you spoken to someone recently in a way that was not loving? *Confess* this sin.

. . . .

. . . .

. . . .

. . . .

. . . .

. . . .

. . . .

. . . .

. . . .

. . . .

. . . .

Simon Peter said unto him, Lord, whither goest thou? Jesus answered him, Whither I go, thou canst not follow me now; but thou shalt follow me afterwards.

Peter said unto him, Lord, why cannot I follow thee now? I will lay down my life for thy sake.

Jesus answered him, Wilt thou lay down thy life for my sake? Verily, verily, I say unto thee, The cock shall not crow, till thou hast denied me thrice.

DAY 21 - **HE IS STRONG**

Peter was a loyal disciple of Jesus. He wanted to follow him, dedicate his life to him, and be strong for his Lord. But here Jesus put Peter face to face with his own inability and weakness. He told Peter that before the day was done, Peter would deny him three times. Though Peter confessed that he would lay down his life for Jesus, when confronted with the threat of persecution, he would display behavior that was anything but faithful to his Lord. He was not alone in this weakness. When Jesus was arrested, all his disciples would abandon him in fear.

"Jesus Loves Me" was probably one of the first Christian songs that you learned as a child. But the simple truth found in the lyrics of this song is not just for children. The line "they are weak, but he is strong" also applies to teenagers, adults, and elderly saints. Despite our best intentions, we are all weak and susceptible to falling into sin. Every time we sin, it is a betrayal and denial of our Lord and Savior.

The failure of Jesus' disciples to remain faithful to him ought to remind us of our own failure to obey God as we should. We are all capable of sin—even great, terrible sins. We should never look at a sin someone else has committed and pridefully think, "I would never do that!" Instead, we must humbly fall on our knees before our heavenly Father. We know that it is only by his power that we can remain faithful to him.

We may be weak, sinful humans. But we belong to a God of unlimited strength. As he proclaimed to his people in the Old Testament, "Behold, I am the LORD, the God of all flesh: is there any thing too hard for me?" (Jer. 32:27). We cannot resist the temptation of sin by our own strength. We must rely on the power of Christ instead (2 Cor. 12:9–10).

ASK YOURSELF...

How can you rely on God's strength when faced with a temptation instead of trying to deal with it on your own?

....

....

....

....

PRAYING TO YOUR HEAVENLY FATHER

- *Praise* God for his omnipotence—his unlimited power.
- *Confess* when you have tried to rely on your own power instead of his.
- *Ask* him to give you the strength to resist the attacks of Satan.

....

....

....

....

....

....

....

....

....

....

....

JOHN 14:1–3

Let not your heart be troubled: ye believe in God, believe also in me.

In my Father's house are many mansions: if it were not so, I would have told you. I go to prepare a place for you.

And if I go and prepare a place for you, I will come again, and receive you unto myself; that where I am, there ye may be also.

DAY 22 – **A HOME IN HEAVEN**

Jesus' disciples were troubled. He had announced that one of them would betray him. He had told them again that he was going away, and they could not go with him. He had just told Peter that he would deny him. The disciples were distressed at the thought of Jesus leaving them and anxious about the events that Jesus was saying would happen in the future. But as Jesus was gathered together with these beloved disciples in the upper room, he brought them comfort. He began, "Let not your heart be troubled" (v. 1).

What comforts the children of God when they are in distress? What calms the fear and anxiety that you may have about the future? The rest of verse 1 tells us the answer: "Ye believe in God, believe also in me." The answer is faith—true faith, that knows your heavenly Father and trusts that he will keep his promises!

Jesus promises here that although he was going away, it was for the purpose of preparing a place for his beloved friends in heaven. This would not be a temporary place, but a permanent dwelling—a home for eternity. And the best part about this forever home is that it is with Jesus. Do you believe this?

Though the disciples were troubled concerning what was about to happen, Jesus instructed them to take comfort in the promise that they would someday be with him forever. This same promise comes to you as well! 2 Corinthians 4:17–18 reminds us to keep this eternal perspective when we face difficulties in our earthly life: "For our light affliction, which is but for a moment, worketh for us a far more exceeding and eternal weight of glory; while we look not at the things which are seen, but at the things which are not seen: for the things which are seen are temporal; but the things which are not seen are eternal."

ASK YOURSELF...

What is troubling your heart today?

. . . .

. . . .

. . . .

. . . .

Have you brought your troubles to God in prayer? Or have you been trying to cope with them on your own?

. . . .

. . . .

. . . .

. . . .

PRAYING TO YOUR HEAVENLY FATHER

- *Praise* God for his constant care and comfort.
- *Thank* him for preparing a home for you in heaven.
- Tell him what is troubling you. *Ask* him to work peace in your heart.

. . . .

. . . .

. . . .

. . . .

. . . .

. . . .

. . . .

. . . .

. . . .

. . . .

. . . .

And whither I go ye know, and the way ye know.

Thomas saith unto him, Lord, we know not whither thou goest; and how can we know the way?

Jesus saith unto him, I am the way, the truth, and the life: no man cometh unto the Father, but by me.

If ye had known me, ye should have known my Father also: and from henceforth ye know him, and have seen him.

Philip saith unto him, Lord, show us the Father, and it sufficeth us.

Jesus saith unto him, Have I been so long time with you, and yet hast thou not known me, Philip? he that hath seen me hath seen the Father; and how sayest thou then, Show us the Father?

Believest thou not that I am in the Father, and the Father in me? the words that I speak unto you I speak not of myself: but the Father that dwelleth in me, he doeth the works.

Believe me that I am in the Father, and the Father in me: or else believe me for the very works' sake.

DAY 23 - **THE ONLY WAY**

After Jesus brought his disciples the comforting truth that he was preparing a place for them in heaven, he assured them that they knew where he was going and they knew the way to get there. But Thomas' interjection shows that they were still confused. So Jesus responded plainly, "I am the way, the truth, and the life" (v. 6). What did he mean by this?

Jesus is the way because the only way that we are able to truly know God and live with him forever is through his death and resurrection. Jesus is the truth because he is the revelation of the Father, who is truth. Jesus is the life because he earned eternal life for us through his work on the cross, and he works this life in us. As Peter would later confess in Acts 4:12, "Neither is there salvation in any other: for there is none other name under heaven given among men, whereby we must be saved."

But at this time, the disciples were uncertain about his words. Philip spoke up and asked Jesus to show them the Father so they could be sure. Jesus once again told them that he was one with the Father. To see the Son is to see the Father. If they wanted a sign, they need only consider all the works that Jesus did. Who else could have done those things but God himself? Jesus challenged the disciples to believe the truth of who he is—the only way to eternal life with the Father.

Arrogant, narrow-minded, unloving, prejudiced—these are all accusations that will be thrown at you today if you dare to suggest that there is only one way to get to heaven. Social media influencers encourage you to trust in how you can improve yourself. The movies and music that the world produces encourage you to embrace sin if it makes you happy. But there is only one way to be delivered from the condemnation and punishment of hell—the way of repenting from sin, believing, and trusting in Jesus Christ alone for your salvation.

ASK YOURSELF...

What do you spend more time studying—the truth of God's word or the entertainment of the world?

. . . .

. . . .

. . . .

. . . .

PRAYING TO YOUR HEAVENLY FATHER

- Have you believed the lies of the world? *Confess* this sin.
- *Ask* him to help you share the way, the truth, and the life with those who are following the wrong path.
- *Pray* the words of Psalm 25:4–5a: "Shew me thy ways, O Lord; teach me thy paths. Lead me in thy truth, and teach me."

. . . .

. . . .

. . . .

. . . .

. . . .

. . . .

. . . .

. . . .

. . . .

. . . .

. . . .

Verily, verily, I say unto you, He that believeth on me, the works that I do shall he do also; and greater works than these shall he do; because I go unto my Father.

And whatsoever ye shall ask in my name, that will I do, that the Father may be glorified in the Son.

If ye shall ask any thing in my name, I will do it.

If ye love me, keep my commandments.

DAY 24 - **ASK IN MY NAME**

As we continue in John 14, Jesus is still preparing his disciples for what was about to take place after his death and resurrection. The disciples did not understand why Jesus had to leave them. But he was showing them here that, although it would be difficult to lose their dear friend and teacher, it was ultimately for their advantage. The advantages of Jesus' ascension into heaven extend to believers today as well.

The disciples were worried that the ministry of Jesus would come to an end when he left them. But this was not the case. The apostles would continue his work of evangelism, teaching, and acts of mercy long after he went to glory. And the church today continues to do this work as well. Although many people had believed in Jesus during his short time on this earth, his followers will continue to spread the gospel to an even greater number of people until he comes again.

How can followers of Jesus carry out this difficult calling? First, after he ascended into heaven, he gave his Spirit to all believers. As weak, sinful humans, we could never imitate Jesus' works without the power of his Spirit in us. We will learn more about this work of the Spirit over the next few days. Second, Jesus promises that we may pray to God for help. Since Jesus died on our behalf, rose, and now sits at the right hand of God in glory, we may ask anything in his name.

Does this mean that we may ask for anything we want in our prayers and God will give it to us? Of course not. Verse 15 reminds us that we must not pray contrary to God's commands. 1 John 5:14 teaches similarly that we must pray according to God's will, not our own desires. But we can be confident that our heavenly Father will give us everything that we need to serve and glorify him if we ask in Jesus' name.

ASK YOURSELF...

What does it mean to pray according to God's will?

....

....

....

....

How do you do this in your prayers?

....

....

....

....

PRAYING TO YOUR HEAVENLY FATHER

- *Thank* God for his gracious gift of prayer.
- Have you prayed contrary to God's will? *Confess* this sin.
- *Ask* for the strength and confidence to share your faith with others.

....

....

....

....

....

....

....

....

....

....

....

And I will pray the Father, and he shall give you another Comforter, that he may abide with you for ever;

Even the Spirit of truth; whom the world cannot receive, because it seeth him not, neither knoweth him: but ye know him; for he dwelleth with you, and shall be in you.

I will not leave you comfortless: I will come to you.

DAY 25 – **THE COMFORTER**

Because the Holy Spirit is one of the three persons of the triune God, knowing about him is just as important as knowing about the Father and the Son. Jesus' promises to his disciples in these verses explain many key truths about the Holy Spirit. Jesus will continue to teach about the work of the Spirit in the coming chapters, so it is worth pausing here to make sure you have a good understanding of the Spirit.

The Holy Spirit is fully God. We see from Genesis 1:2 that he is eternal and was present at creation. Do you remember reading in John 3:33 that God is true? We recently considered John 14:6, where Jesus calls himself "the truth." Here verse 17 refers to the Spirit of truth, emphasizing that the Holy Spirit is inseparable from the Father and the Son. He proceeds from the Father and the Son and testifies to them.

Verse 17 also points out that the Holy Spirit is uniquely present in believers. In the Old Testament, only some believers, such as the prophets, were given the Spirit fully. But in the New Testament since Pentecost, God graciously gives all believers the Spirit in their hearts. The Spirit puts the new life of Christ in the heart of an elect sinner and continually works to make the believer more like Christ (Titus 3:5).

Why else is the Spirit's presence important? Jesus had been physically present with his disciples to comfort them. But now he was going away. However, he would not leave them comfortless (v. 18). After his ascension into heaven, he would give them "another Comforter"—the Holy Spirit. Although Jesus would soon be leaving them in body, he would still be with them in Spirit. He is with you in Spirit, too! As the Heidelberg Catechism teaches in Question and Answer 49, the presence of the Spirit in the heart of the believer gives us comfort now and is also a promise that Jesus will come back again someday.

ASK YOURSELF...

How often do you spend quiet time in prayer or meditating on God's word?

....
....
....
....

Could making more time for this help you experience the comfort of the Holy Spirit more?

....
....
....
....

PRAYING TO YOUR HEAVENLY FATHER

- *Praise* God for his graciousness—that he gives us gifts and benefits that we do not deserve.
- *Thank* him for the gift of the Spirit.
- *Ask* him to bring comfort to your heart by the power of the Spirit.

....
....
....
....
....
....
....
....
....
....
....

Yet a little while, and the world seeth me no more; but ye see me: because I live, ye shall live also.

At that day ye shall know that I am in my Father, and ye in me, and I in you.

He that hath my commandments, and keepeth them, he it is that loveth me: and he that loveth me shall be loved of my Father, and I will love him, and will manifest myself to him.

Judas saith unto him, not Iscariot, Lord, how is it that thou wilt manifest thyself unto us, and not unto the world?

Jesus answered and said unto him, If a man love me, he will keep my words: and my Father will love him, and we will come unto him, and make our abode with him.

He that loveth me not keepeth not my sayings: and the word which ye hear is not mine, but the Father's which sent me.

DAY 26 – **COMMUNION WITH GOD**

In the upper room, Jesus continued to explain to his beloved disciples the benefits they would receive from his going away. Yesterday we learned that he would give them his Spirit to comfort them. Today we read of another benefit—deeper communion with God. The disciples would not have Jesus with them for much longer, but they would soon have a closer relationship with God through the Holy Spirit in their hearts.

The Father, Son, and Holy Spirit exist in a relationship of perfect love. As an adopted child of God, you are able to be a part of this relationship because God loves you. God loves his children so much that he sent his only begotten Son to die for their sins so that this relationship could be restored. He is happy to have a close, personal relationship with you.

Because God loves you, you love him. It is important to keep these in the correct order. If you love God, you will keep his commandments. God is holy, meaning he is undefiled by sin and unable to be in the presence of sin. He cannot dwell with one who is not keeping his commandments. Our fellowship with God is possible only through the work of Christ on our behalf.

If you are living in unrepentant sin, you will often feel as though God is far away from you. You may find it difficult to pray. You may also find yourself not really listening to your pastor on Sunday or avoiding reading God's word because you do not want to be reminded of your sin. But God never leaves you! He will often use your conscience or the rebuke of a fellow Christian to draw you back to him.

Fellowship with God will be the most wonderful thing about heaven. Revelation 21:3 promises that in the new Jerusalem, "the tabernacle of God is with men, and he will dwell with them, and they shall be his people, and God himself shall be with them, and be their God." Someday we will rejoice to be in the presence of God without any sin to separate us from him.

ASK YOURSELF...

Has your sin ever made you feel far away from God?

....

....

....

....

PRAYING TO YOUR HEAVENLY FATHER

- *Praise* God for his majesty and justice.
- *Thank* him for bringing you into covenant fellowship with him.
- *Ask* him to help you follow his commandments to show your love for him.

....

....

....

....

....

....

....

....

....

....

....

These things have I spoken unto you, being yet present with you.

But the Comforter, which is the Holy Ghost, whom the Father will send in my name, he shall teach you all things, and bring all things to your remembrance, whatsoever I have said unto you.

Peace I leave with you, my peace I give unto you: not as the world giveth, give I unto you. Let not your heart be troubled, neither let it be afraid.

Ye have heard how I said unto you, I go away, and come again unto you. If ye loved me, ye would rejoice, because I said, I go unto the Father: for my Father is greater than I.

And now I have told you before it come to pass, that, when it is come to pass, ye might believe.

Hereafter I will not talk much with you: for the prince of this world cometh, and hath nothing in me.

But that the world may know that I love the Father; and as the Father gave me commandment, even so I do. Arise, let us go hence.

DAY 27 – **COMFORTER AND TEACHER**

E ven on the night before his death, Jesus was selflessly focused on comforting his disciples. He told them that he would prepare a place for them in heaven and provide the way to get there. He assured them that he would hear their prayers. He promised to give them his Spirit so that he could comfort them and dwell with them. Here he showed them another way that the Spirit would give them comfort—by being their teacher.

Have you ever noticed the difference between the disciples in the gospels and in the book of Acts? While they were learning from Jesus during his earthly ministry, they did not completely understand the truth of what he was teaching. We can see from the questions that they asked him that they were often uncertain about who he was and what he was going to do. But these same disciples gave great and knowledgeable confessions of faith when they went out to preach the gospel in the book of Acts. Many of them also wrote parts of the Bible. What changed?

The difference came from having the Holy Spirit in their hearts as a teacher. Jesus had been their teacher while he was with them, but now the Spirit would take on that role. As the Spirit of Jesus, he teaches the truth of the Son of God. He not only brings comfort but empowers and enables a child of God to run the race that he has prepared for him on this earth with endurance (Heb. 12:1). The same Spirit that taught the disciples is present in every believer today.

Have you ever been reading the Bible or listening to a sermon and made a connection in your mind to something else that you have learned or experienced? That is the Spirit working in your heart as a teacher. Have you ever remembered something about God that brought you comfort in a moment when you were struggling? That is the Spirit reminding you of the truth. The peace that comes from this truth cannot be found in anything the world has to offer.

ASK YOURSELF...

How does knowing that the Spirit is a teacher encourage you in your own study of the Bible?

....
....
....
....

PRAYING TO YOUR HEAVENLY FATHER

- *Praise* God for always keeping his promises.
- *Thank* him for the gift of the Spirit as a teacher.
- *Ask* him to work true peace in your heart.

....
....
....
....
....
....
....
....
....
....
....

I am the true vine, and my Father is the husbandman.

Every branch in me that beareth not fruit he taketh away: and every branch that beareth fruit, he purgeth it, that it may bring forth more fruit.

Now ye are clean through the word which I have spoken unto you.

Abide in me, and I in you. As the branch cannot bear fruit of itself, except it abide in the vine; no more can ye, except ye abide in me.

DAY 28 – **THE TRUE VINE**

Jesus turns to the picture of a vine to teach his disciples about the relationship between himself and his people. Grapevines were a familiar sight in the land of Israel. In the Old Testament, Israel was referred to as God's chosen vine. They were called to bear fruit for his glory (Ps. 80:8–16; Jer. 2:21). But as you know, they failed to do this over and over again, and God had cut them off by sending them into captivity.

All hope was not lost. We read of God's promises of restoration throughout the Old Testament prophecies (see Hos. 14:7 and Zech. 8:12). He would someday bring life back to the withered vine and make it flourish once again. From the stump of this vine came Jesus—the true vine (Is. 11:1).

Where Israel failed in being a fruitful vine, Jesus perfectly accomplished what they could not do. By grace, all of God's children are grafted, or implanted, into him. This life-giving connection to the true vine gives us spiritual life. The vine enables us to bear the fruit of good works for the glory of God, and being engrafted to him ensures that we will do so (see Heidelberg Catechism Q&A 64).

God is the husbandman who maintains this vine. He cuts off the branches that do not bear fruit. He also prunes the ones who do bear fruit so that they will produce more. Sometimes he does this by sending trials that take away what we have been trusting in—instead of God—to strengthen our faith in him. Another way we are pruned when we are walking in sin is through admonitions from God's word or from other believers. This is a hard but necessary process for spiritual growth.

We cannot flourish apart from Christ because we cannot bear any fruit apart from him. But the fruit that we bear is a sign of his life in us. This fruit is obeying God's commandments, loving God, and loving others. Bearing this fruit brings glory to the vine and the farmer, not to the individual branch.

ASK YOURSELF...

How has God "pruned" you lately?

....

....

....

....

PRAYING TO YOUR HEAVENLY FATHER

- *Praise* God for his covenant faithfulness to his people.
- *Thank* him for the gift of spiritual life in Christ.
- *Ask* him to work in your heart and life so that you bear fruit for his glory.

....

....

....

....

....

....

....

....

....

....

....

I am the vine, ye are the branches: He that abideth in me, and I in him, the same bringeth forth much fruit: for without me ye can do nothing.

If a man abide not in me, he is cast forth as a branch, and is withered; and men gather them, and cast them into the fire, and they are burned.

If ye abide in me, and my words abide in you, ye shall ask what ye will, and it shall be done unto you.

Herein is my Father glorified, that ye bear much fruit; so shall ye be my disciples.

As the Father hath loved me, so have I loved you: continue ye in my love.

If ye keep my commandments, ye shall abide in my love; even as I have kept my Father's commandments, and abide in his love.

These things have I spoken unto you, that my joy might remain in you, and that your joy might be full.

DAY 29 – **ABIDING IN CHRIST**

In the passage that you read yesterday, Jesus introduced the idea of abiding in Christ to his disciples. In the verses that you read today, he expands on that by showing three different, but related ways that his people can abide in him—by abiding in Christ, by his words abiding in us, and by abiding in his love. These are true for every one of his children.

Do you know what it means to abide? The idea of this term is to remain, or stay in one place, to live there permanently. The believer abides in Christ by faith. By faith, God's people know and trust him for their salvation. By faith, they depend on him for their spiritual life and growth. By faith, they experience the benefits of being united with Christ. By faith, they have a close, personal relationship with him. This faith is a gift of God that the Holy Spirit works in the hearts of all his elect.

Jesus also talks about his words abiding in you. What does he mean by this? Jesus had given his disciples much instruction on how to live as followers of Christ. With these words in their hearts, they knew what their calling was and were able to pray for what they needed to carry out this calling. Jesus' instruction in John and in all of God's word comes to you as well. If his words abide in you, you will know how you should live and how to pray for the strength to follow his instruction.

Finally, Jesus says to abide in his love. If you truly believe that he loves you, and you are reminded daily of this love by abiding in his word, what other response could you have than to live according to God's commands? Abiding in Christ's love means that you show that love to those around you. A life of bearing fruit for God's glory is a life full of joy, a true joy that living only for yourself can never give you.

ASK YOURSELF...

How could sin or dwelling on your trials keep you from abiding in Christ?

....

....

....

....

PRAYING TO YOUR HEAVENLY FATHER

- *Thank* God that we can put our trust in him.
- *Ask* him to help you live a life of abiding in Christ.
- *Praise* him for the patience that he shows to his people.

....

....

....

....

....

....

....

....

....

....

....

....

This is my commandment, That ye love one another, as I have loved you.

Greater love hath no man than this, that a man lay down his life for his friends.

Ye are my friends, if ye do whatsoever I command you.

Henceforth I call you not servants; for the servant knoweth not what his lord doeth: but I have called you friends; for all things that I have heard of my Father I have made known unto you.

Ye have not chosen me, but I have chosen you, and ordained you, that ye should go and bring forth fruit, and that your fruit should remain: that whatsoever ye shall ask of the Father in my name, he may give it you.

These things I command you, that ye love one another.

DAY 30 – **FRIENDS OF GOD**

What is a friend? A friend is someone whom you love and care about. A friend is someone whom you know well and talk to often. You are excited to share things with him or her. You tell a friend things that you would not tell just anyone. Friends also spend time together and enjoy each other's company. You want to hang out with your friends whenever you can. You are excited to see them!

In the Old Testament, Abraham was called a friend of God (Is. 41:8). Jesus extended this same privilege to his disciples. He also has this relationship of friendship with every single believer by his Spirit. It is extraordinary that the eternal and all-powerful Creator of the universe would consider us not just to be his servants, but his friends!

He loves and cares for you. He knows you and enjoys it when you spend time reading and thinking about his word. He is happy when you spend time talking to him in prayer. Do you have the same desire to talk to God and spend time in fellowship with him? Or do you value time with your earthly friends more and push your time with your heavenly Father to the back burner?

Abraham showed that he was a friend of God by following God's commands. Jesus repeats the same idea in verse 14 of this chapter. If you are a friend of God, you are called to love those around you. Loving others is the essence of following his commands. Jesus showed just how much he loves you by sacrificing his life for you. Would you be willing to do this for any of your friends? Are you willing to serve them and help any of your friends when they are in need? Or are you interested only in what they can do for you?

ASK YOURSELF...

How can you show that you are a friend of God?

....

....

....

....

How can you be a better friend to those around you?

....

....

....

....

PRAYING TO YOUR HEAVENLY FATHER

- *Thank* him for calling you a friend.
- Have you been neglecting your relationship with God? *Confess* this sin.
- *Ask* him to help you show love in your earthly friendships.

....

....

....

....

....

....

....

....

....

....

....

If the world hate you, ye know that it hated me before it hated you.

If ye were of the world, the world would love his own: but because ye are not of the world, but I have chosen you out of the world, therefore the world hateth you.

Remember the word that I said unto you, The servant is not greater than his lord. If they have persecuted me, they will also persecute you; if they have kept my saying, they will keep yours also.

But all these things will they do unto you for my name's sake, because they know not him that sent me.

If I had not come and spoken unto them, they had not had sin: but now they have no cloak for their sin.

He that hateth me hateth my Father also.

If I had not done among them the works which none other man did, they had not had sin: but now have they both seen and hated both me and my Father.

But this cometh to pass, that the word might be fulfilled that is written in their law, They hated me without a cause.

But when the Comforter is come, whom I will send unto you from the Father, even the Spirit of truth, which proceedeth from the Father, he shall testify of me:

And ye also shall bear witness, because ye have been with me from the beginning.

DAY 31 – **HATED BY THE WORLD**

The world will hate you. This is a hard truth that Jesus stated plainly to his disciples. It is true for all believers. He had given them a great deal of comfort because he was going away, but he also now gives them a caution: being a friend of God will make you an enemy of the world.

When Jesus refers to "the world" here, he is talking about society in general. Society is made up of a majority of ungodly people who are hostile to Christ and Christians. They hate Christians because Christians are different from them. They hate Christ because he is the light that shows them they are walking in darkness.

They demonstrate this hatred by persecuting you and all those who show themselves to be friends of God. This persecution can take various forms. It could be an unbeliever who mocks you to the point of verbal assault or unbelieving family or friends who shun you. It could be the loss of a job or attacks on your business in the form of fines or lawsuits. It could even be physical harm, imprisonment, or death. Most of the disciples to whom Jesus was speaking here would die a martyr's death.

The world's hatred of Jesus would soon be revealed when they would commit the great sin of crucifying Christ. But we know that God had a divine purpose even in this sin. The actions of the ungodly would accomplish our salvation and bring glory to God. The persecution that you will endure in your life is also under the control of God and accomplishes his purposes.

How can you endure this hatred? How can you continue to live in this world that is growing increasingly wicked and hostile? How can you dare to share the gospel with others in this environment? It will be difficult. But Jesus reminds his disciples once again that they will have the Spirit in their hearts to comfort and enable them to carry out their calling faithfully. He gives these gifts of the Spirit to you, too.

ASK YOURSELF...

How have you experienced hatred from the world?

....

....

....

....

What was your response?

....

....

....

....

PRAYING TO YOUR HEAVENLY FATHER

- *Thank* God for preserving his church, even in times of intense persecution.
- Have you tried to avoid the hatred of the world by hiding your faith? *Confess* this sin.
- *Ask* him to give you strength to endure the hatred of the world.

....

....

....

....

....

....

....

....

....

....

....

DEVOTIONS ON
THE GOSPEL OF JOHN FOR TEENS

Read them all!

These four 1-month devotionals follow Jesus' ministry as relayed by the apostle John. Each devotional emphasizes the importance of confessing that Jesus Christ is God and also provides much practical application to teen readers.

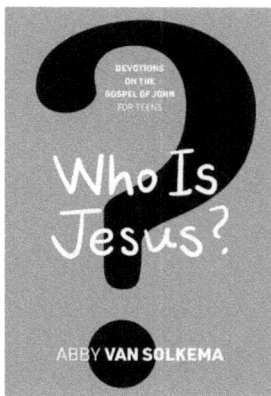

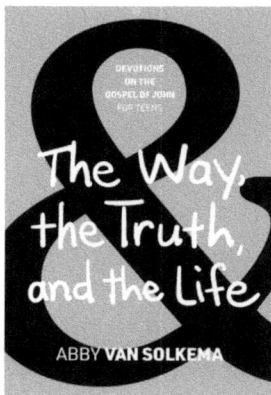

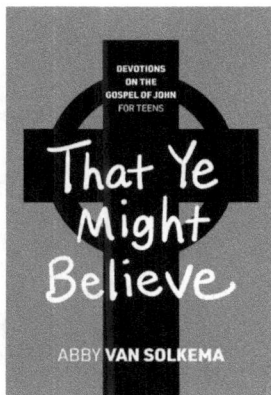

DEVOTIONS ON THE GOSPEL OF JOHN FOR TEENS

Who Is Jesus?

ABBY VAN SOLKEMA

DEVOTIONS ON THE GOSPEL OF JOHN FOR TEENS

Humble Servant

ABBY VAN SOLKEMA

DEVOTIONS ON THE GOSPEL OF JOHN FOR TEENS

The Way, the Truth, and the Life

ABBY VAN SOLKEMA

DEVOTIONS ON THE GOSPEL OF JOHN FOR TEENS

That Ye Might Believe

ABBY VAN SOLKEMA

Available at rfpa.org

www.ingramcontent.com/pod-product-compliance
Lightning Source LLC
Chambersburg PA
CBHW072357090426
42741CB00012B/3060